Trust Yourself

I0224020

Alexandria R Wesley

chipmunkapublishing
the mental health publisher

All rights reserved, no part of this publication may be reproduced by any means, electronic, mechanical photocopying, documentary, film or in any other format without prior written permission of the publisher.

Published by
Chipmunkapublishing
PO Box 6872
Brentwood
Essex CM13 1ZT
United Kingdom

http://www.chipmunkapublishing.com

Copyright © Alexandria R Wesley 2010

Edited by Aleks Lech

Chipmunkapublishing gratefully acknowledge the support of Arts Council England.

Trust Yourself

Dedicated to the kids.

Alexandria R Wesley

Trust Yourself

I, Alex, was born in Lansing MI, in 1963. I live there now with my husband Dan and 2 cats and a service dog.

I grew up depressed and suicidal, but hide it well by laughing and smiling all the time. Nobody noticed. Finally in college after seeing several different therapists... I was diagnosed with Obsessive Compulsive Disorder. We also discovered the abuse. I have been on psych meds for the OCD ever since-they have helped a lot! They dampen down the anxiety.

Now days I enjoy my husband and my animals and dream for a future when I can have my house in the country .... with a horse named later.

Alexandria R Wesley

Trust Yourself

Prologue

I am an incest survivor. I was sexually abused by my respected church leader father.* I am also a survivor of satanic ritual abuse. I believe my whole family was involved in that. As a child I was forced to take part in many rituals as my family worshiped Satan. We had banquets where we ate people, where we ate babies. I watched my son die as a sacrifice. Many times I thought I would be killed. I was also forced to abuse others. These poems were written over seven years as I learned these things about my family and myself, as I learned the history that I was brought up to believe wasn't true. I also learned that I am a lot stronger than I ever imagined I could be. A lot stronger than my family ever let me believe. The poems are not in chronological order. I just put them in the order that felt right, that I hoped would make sense. I can't prove any of this is true, but I believe it is. I hope that as you read these poems you will realise that sexual abuse and especially cult abuse takes place. Maybe you will see that it happens even in churches, even in respectable homes. Maybe once people realise that it happens, they (you) will start to notice when things are not quite right and we can start to end it so that other little girls and boys won't be forced to live through it. Very possibly you will realise that you have lived through the same things. My memories may trigger some of your own. Your life will start to make sense. Then you will know that you are not alone. And if you need help, you can get it.

*names have been changed.

"You know the truth," my therapist said. "You know it inside your self."

I hated it when she said that. I wanted her to give me an answer now. What she was talking about meant I'd have to learn to trust my instincts. That was something that I found very difficult after growing up in a "wonderful Christian" home that I felt was hiding sexual abuse. I was often pulled back to this question. Were my memories true? My father denied the abuse and my mom and rest of the family had run to his defense and left me on the outside. It was very hard and left me wondering if my memories were true. So I often debated it with myself in my head.

I was 24 years old, in college at Michigan State University majoring in psychology and taking any class that looked interesting. I was floating; most of my energy was going to my therapy. I was in school mostly because I found it easier than working full time. In my family it was one or the other. I didn't know what I wanted to be when I grew up. So I was in school and, unbeknown to my family, I had started therapy. During therapy I realized that my dad had sexually abused me.

I didn't want to believe that my dad had done such a horrible thing to me, but yet I also believed myself. I had spent so much time over the years trying to get somebody to help me. I'd been asking for help, sometimes in blatant ways, sometimes in unconscious ways. I had often become depressed, had even attempted suicide. I had found growing up to be a very difficult experience. I had started therapy to try and understand myself. And now I was finding answers, just not answers that I wanted.

As a child I had often been a worrier and had a lot of

stomach aches that my dad referred to as a worrier's stomach. The depression had started most seriously in High School. I remember one week in my senior year, realizing how seriously I was thinking about killing myself, that I scared myself. All these symptoms add to my belief that I'm right.

After graduation, I went away to a Christian school and struggled with a lot of depression there too. But I enjoyed being away from my family and was sad to have to move back home after college graduation. I needed to move out of my father's house but felt that was impossible. This was not something my parents encouraged either. They wanted me home. I often complained to friends that I wanted to run away from home. One friend commented that, as I was an adult, I didn't need to run away, I should just move out. But for some reason it didn't feel possible to me.

I was still in school taking classes, partially because my dad wanted me to. Another friend of mine was trying to convince me to go to a counsellor. We argued about it often. I thought about her arguments and I talked to God about it. I had seen counsellors in the past; it had never gone well. I had many reasons why it hadn't worked in the past and wouldn't help me now. I told God I would go back to therapy if five things happened. My parents couldn't know about it, I had to be not living at home. It had to be free, the therapist had to be a lady, and she had to be a Christian. I knew those stipulations would never come true, if only because I couldn't afford to move out of the house. About a week later dad told me he would pay for me to move into the dorm at school, so that I wouldn't have to drive through the winter weather. I was absolutely shocked! The one thing I KNEW wouldn't happen had happened!

It took about a month to get into the dorm. I still put off getting a counsellor, but finally I found one that fit most of my criteria. I couldn't find one that was free, but did find one that was cheap.

Therapy was so good for me. It was what I needed. Honestly, looking back on it now, even without starting to deal with the sexual abuse, to me it seems incredible, the things I learned. I worked hard. It was very difficult.

I've always wondered why I needed the therapy. Why wasn't I able to move out till I got into therapy? I know my parents loved me. Why didn't they see I needed to get out on my own? I guess it's just hard sometimes to give others what they need even when it hurts. The problem is that the way I ended up doing it ripped me out of my family and now we can hardly even be friends because I hurt them so badly.

I couldn't remember the abuse till I got into therapy. That was the first time I felt safe and the first time that somebody actually listened to me.

My parents always used to tell me I kept them young. I was the youngest of a very big family. After I started therapy and started to finally feel like a grown up, I worried that I wasn't keeping them young any more. Then one day I was talking to my mom and the topic came up and she said I was keeping her young. As we talked, I realised that she always looked at me as someone that needed to be taken care of either by her or by my family or by a husband. That is sad, that she couldn't see that I could take care of myself. I wish she had lived to see me now that I take care of others.

I got several part time jobs, because I didn't like working in one job all day. So instead I worked two or three different jobs. I worked in the MSU library, in book repair. I did yard work and cleaned houses. I enjoyed it. I occasionally did portraits in pastels for people and made money that way. I found ways to support myself that were very different from my family. I was trying to find myself separately from my family. This was very important

After about two years in therapy I looked at my finances and how I was getting along with the family. I decided to move out of the house. I told my parents what I wanted to do. They were very against it, and afraid; they felt it was dangerous to live in E Lansing. But I convinced them that there was a good lock on my bedroom door and gradually they accepted that I was going to do it.

I was happy to move out. But it was scary. What if I couldn't afford it? And it has been very hard to live on my own. I went from an upper class life style in my dad's house to almost the bottom of the economic ladder. I've never made enough money to live at the same level as I came from. And I do miss the higher standard of living. But I have always had a roof over my head, and never starved. Plus I am happier, and that is most important.

Over time, I'm learning growing and finally becoming an

adult. And it isn't half as bad as I thought it would be. I'm learning to live my life as I want to and that that is OK. Life is about learning to trust yourself to take care of yourself, to trust your instincts. And live.

GOOD GUYS WEAR WHITE

Good guys wear white
Bad guys were black
That is the was it's supposed to be.
Mommy is hurting me
She's sticking a metal stick in my vagina
Mommy is a good guy
Mommy wears white.
Mommy is a good guy?
But Mommy hurts me
She says she loves me
But what she does feels bad/wrong
I must be a bad girl
Bad little girl
I'll be good
So then Mommy won't hurt me
I'll be best
Mommy still hurts me.
I'm sorry Mommy
Who is Good?
Who is wearing the white hat?
Who is wearing the black hat?
Its always been easy
Mommy and daddy wear white
They are good
What they do is good
A fact
What do you do when
daddy rapes you?
Who wears the white hat?
Good guys wear white.
Everybody knows that!
In fairy tales you can always tell who the bad guys are.
The good buys wear white
teachers, preachers,
mom and dad

bad guys wear black
strangers...
In all my worst nightmares the definite lines blur and I
don't know
Who are the bad guys?!
My worst nightmares have become reality
and I don't know who to trust any more.
Good guys wear white
Who is wearing white?!
I'm confused. I'm lost
Where is the white?!
The rules have changed
Good guys wear white
Bad guys wear black
Good guys wear black
Bad guys wear white
Good guys black wear
Guys bad white wear
Wear black white guys
Who is wearing white?

Trust Yourself

I am a space alien
I was dropped into this world
and told to relate to humans
I am not a human
I don't understand them
I don't understand their feelings
I don't know how to relate to them.
I'm not sure they are worth trying to relate to
I'm not sure they are worth
trying to understand
I am a space alien.

God, thank you for Jamie
for her love despite all the stupid things I do
she keeps listening
she doesn't condemn
she holds me
she never gets mad
You give her such patience and strength
she is always a calm voice on the other end of the phone
telling me she still loves me
telling me she is still there
showing me that You are still there
she points me to You, God
she is showing me Your love when otherwise I couldn't see You
she loves me like You do
she says it's Your love through her
Thank You for her
she holds my hand
she hugs me
she'd let me cry--if I would
she lets me feel
she wants me to heal
she loves me
amazing
there were no words for what this means to me
she loves me
The world isn't as scary when seen from her arms.

Trust Yourself

Michigan State beat Northwestern Saturday 76 to 14
Dad raped me.
My old testament teacher talked about Solomon
and his life last week.
Dad made me have oral sex with him.
It snowed last Thursday.
Norma put her tongue in my vagina.
MSU students partied this weekend.
Mom let dad rape me.
I worked on homework all weekend.
Dad raped me.
I have to work tomorrow.
Dad made me have oral sex with him.
Nothing matters--the world just keeps spinning
Nothing stops it from turning
Nothing.

I hate him
I hate him so damn much
never be able to say it enough
I hate him
Woe to anyone who tries to tell me to forgive him
God, you will ask me that won't You
I'm sorry I can't express it (the anger)-the pain
can't
It hurts too damn bad
so bad
so bad
I hate him

They know the truth
yet they hide it
they'd rather
we hurt
I hurt
Than to stop the pain
They'd rather protect themselves
I hate them

He/they strapped me down spread eagle
then he put the metal rod in me.
I hate him
Don't want to forgive him
Don't want to see this from his perspective
He never saw it from mine
Friends say he is old
He never thought about the fact that I was young
He is old, he isn't going change
you, Violet will have to compromise
No.
No.
Do you compromise with a rapist?

Trust Yourself

Bastard Damn him
Do you forgive somebody who
tied you up and......
Damn him.
Do you ask his forgiveness?
Oh, God
Just to have it over
To Bleed
And watch my life drain away
To have peace
To have it all be over
To not have to keep putting one foot in
front of the other
To not have to be strong
not have to be responsible
not have to handle it all
To have it be over
To not have to figure it all out any more
That is what death means to me
To have peace
No more pain
No more struggle
To have it over
Could anybody just hold me right now
To say they understand
the fear and the pain
Not judge
Just understand
The hurt
Just hold me and understand

Friends want me to fight
To keep going
But where are they when I lay in bed
At night waiting for sleep
Knowing daddy is coming to put his fingers in me
When I whisper to God
Please stop him and He doesn't
When I can't sleep
I want to cut for me
For them I can't
But where are they when I'm alone?
When I long for drugs to make me
Sleep, to fog over, not feel.
Where are they when I'm alone

Trust Yourself

I love your arms
I'm safe there
But I can't stay there
I have to leave your office
Have to deal with it all alone

I feel so alone
You all tell me how strong I am
I'm not strong--
I'm a little girl searching desperately for love
Just a little girl alone
Mom I'd forgive you in a second if you'd just
Hold me safe and love me.

We were abused
used for things no person
no animal should be used for
We had our childhood stolen from us
Somehow we survived
And lived to tell about it
Then people didn't believe us
We are called crazy, sick, delusional
I break from my family
Why? I don't know
(I don't know)
I didn't know what I was doing
It would be so easy
to go back
God why..when I've already
lost so much
Why am I required to lose even more?
Why do I have to pay the price?
Why do I have to lose my family?
I've already given up so much,
Why is it the victim who pays the prices?

Trust Yourself

Alone
Dark, empty, abyss
Alone
To fight the ghosts
Alone
Nobody there to help
Alone
Facing the pain
Alone
It's almost too much to handle
It is too much to handle
I'm alone
All alone
Again

I drag myself out of my bed.
I can't believe it's morning.
I hate morning.
Time to get dressed and drag myself through
another day of work and school.
One more day to survive.
I head out the door to go to class.
I know I have to pretend to be a student.
Have to let Mom and Dad think I don't know.
Have to pretend to be a responsible adult.
I have to pretend to care about life,
while I watch mine fall apart.
While I find out everything I've ever
believed about my family is wrong.
I have to pretend I don't know the truth,
that I don't know dad raped me.
Pretend that it doesn't matter.
Pretend
I hate it.

Trust Yourself

I had a baby
I had a little boy
His name is Peter
I love him
My little boy
Peter

He had blond curly hair,
He was so beautiful
He was so beautiful
I help him
I nursed him
My baby
My beautiful baby

I call him Peter
His father was my brother, Peter.
He looked like Peter,
so I named him that
the day I remembered him.

They broke his neck like a chicken
Why couldn't I save him?!
Did Satan want him too?
Didn't he get enough?
he got so many!

He is an angel with Jesus now
Thank You God for taking care of my little boy
My little baby
I love you Peter.
I love you so much.
The Bastards killed him!
I say they don't know how to be real
-they are plastic
But I am plastic too

I am afraid to be real

God, it's so lonely
You all tell me to act like an adult
But nobody told me how
They say it's my choice
But not really
If it was my choice
It would be settled
Therapists
She isn't my therapist
You, Jamie, are the only one allowed to play therapist.

Trust Yourself

Can't go on
So how do you?
I send a stick figure out in my place
She walks and talks and works
But she is empty
Just a shell
A stick figure with nothing inside
Can't hurt her because there is nothing to hurt.

Sometimes I can feel the Rage
that must be inside of me
Most the time it's just
numbness, nothingness
When I think of mom
It's like I have to forgive her
What could she do?
But maybe it's...
I was/am nothing
I have no right to have feelings
How can you be angry when you don't exist?

Trust Yourself

I feel like I'm standing alone against the cult
I have chosen to follow God and to leave the cult
To do what is right
I have no family
I have to survive on my own
I have to fight the cult
I have given up my family
I have nothing left
I am alone
I hate it
It hurts
Alone again
But isn't that how it's always been?

Lauri has family
Jamie has family
Chris has family
Seems like everybody has family
......I.....
To have somebody who
I'm the most important to
I no longer have anybody who would drop anything for me
Not that I don't have friends...
And maybe I expect too much.
I just ... wish.
Feel lonely...
Alone
My whole life - I've been alone

Does anybody know how this feels?
This person who told Jamie three hours a week was too much
Have they ever been there?
Do they really understand?

Trust Yourself

Not having enough time
It's like knowing your feelings aren't really important.
Like she doesn't want to know how I feel any more.

Does anybody know the pain I'm in?
I can't seem to express it.
Not to anybody.
Will I survive?
I wonder.
I am an open wound.
So much pain
Incredible pain
Its amazing that I am still standing.
Sometimes it seems like people take it for granted
They get so used to me not falling apart totally
They forget that it's far from easy.
They don't know how hard it is to just keep walking.
I do it because I have to
Do you all know?
Do you all realise?
You get so used to me walking
Do you remember how hard it is?

There is a part of me
that is sure I'm wrong
That lives in fear of being found out
Why is that?
I think
I know I'm right
But dad walks into the room
And I deny it all

I see the circumstantial evidence
I know the feeling inside
that I can't ask forgiveness
I think it's because I'm right
hear this voice that can't give in
she can't give in
she can't apologize
she isn't wrong
I am choosing to listen to her
because it's easier?
easier than asking forgiveness?
when I'm truly not sure?
(she gets angry when I say that)
because she is right
When I believe
then I have the energy to fight
to live
If I don't believe
I can't go on
there will be no reason for me to live.
I think I was put on earth to fight
to start a fight against the cult

Do I live in reality
or a myth?
Where is reality?

Go away world go away!

Trust Yourself

They are too perfect to be wrong.
The kid has to be wrong
Go away people - I hate people
I have to be a daughter, student, room mate
I even have to wake up in the morning and be nice to
people.
They used to call me sunshine
Miss Smiley. Always happy.
Go away! Go away!
I feel like being sad
Sorry mom but I do.
If that makes you all leave me...
I wish you wouldn't
And I'll play any game to stop you,
But I want to be sad.
Like I was never allowed to be sad.
Can I be happy, can I be free?
Unimaginable concept, truly impossible
I can't grow up and be something. Just
Can't, the other option is death.
And I can't die--can't do that to you
Just curl up with my blanket and
my pillow and my night light, stereo,
and my notebook and go to sleep.
Just put my head on your shoulder and relax
Yeah, I do feel safe/good there.
I'm gonna grow up and get better for real.

I have given up my family
I have given up watching Joyce's kids grow up
I have given up seeing Andrew, Wit, Kelly, and Gary.
I can't call them on the phone
I can't wish them happy birthday
I can't hug Andrew any more
I can't play with him any more
I can't take him out for fun any more
I wonder if he will even remember me.
I wonder if Wit will remember me
That I doubt
There is no way I can get those moments back
They are gone forever
They are lost forever
Even if someday I can see those kids again
I have lost their childhoods forever
I will have missed their childhoods.
That can never be returned
That is lost to me forever
And for that I mourn
That hurts more than anybody will ever know.
The price I am paying
God, it is so very, very high.
So high
The price I pay for an ancestor's mistake
The ancestor that chose to follow Satan rather than God
Now I must give so much up to do what is right
That makes me so damn angry
Why am I the one?
Why didn't one of them do it so I wouldn't have to!?!

I can't call Joyce on the phone
I think I have lost two mothers
Mom and Joyce
I miss them

Trust Yourself

What have I lost?
It's big things
and it's little things
who do I put on official forms
as to who to call in an emergency?
Other college kids can call home and
say I need this and they get it
I can't
simple little things
And Big things
No family to come to my graduation
No family to go to for holidays
No father to give me away when I get married
(if I get married and if we are still not speaking)
I don't feel really important to anybody
I am not anybody's family

I can't go home and steal things
I can't even go home and get things I own easily.

Is it so wrong to want some of that?
Is it wrong to want what I had?
I have very little support
At least it feels like it
And nobody who I can really ask for help from.
It hurts
Do you realise how much it hurts?
How much I don't have any more.
People use to ask why I wasn't willing
to cut off from my family
Stupid question!
Think about it folks
How would you feel?!!?
Think about what the cost is.
Think about it

People used to tell me
Just confront your family
Then everything will be OK.
Then you will be happy.
They don't know what they are talking about
Holidays are the hardest
I try to be brave and strong
I try to find things to do
Places to go
People to see
Ways to celebrate
To not just feel sorry for myself
I wonder if you, my closest friend, even really
understand
I don't think you do
Maybe you're right
Maybe it hurts so bad
Because I fight the change so much
Because I'm stuck in the middle
--so it's my own fault!
But you try it!
You try walking away from your family
Give up your parents
Give up your husband
Give up your kids
Every person that
You've loved and cared about all your life
And see how it feels
See if you do it right
See if you don't get stuck in the middle
Try the medicine, Doctor!
Get your heart torn out
See if you don't fight
See if you don't get stuck
Think about it.

Trust Yourself

Friend,
You wonder how to go on
When life feels so impossible.
When you know you can't
possibly take one more step.

All I can tell you is I understand
I want to hold you and keep you safe
I understand how hard it is to keep going
How do you do it?

You lay on your bed
You scream at God
You get mad at friends who tell you
To keep going
You get mad at Jamie.
Because you are the one who has to live
this life and not her,
Not the friends
You pray
You read
You talk on the phone
You get very angry
You get very depressed
You pray for death
You sleep
You work
You go to class
You go talk to Jamie
And somehow
impossibly, even though you know
beyond a shadow of doubt
That you won't,
Even though you know you can't go on
Somehow you do keep living

I remember that Jamie loves me
And believes me
I wonder at that
(how can somebody that neat love me!?)
I think of Andrew,
And know that I have to keep living
Because I have to help him escape

I don't know if this helps at all
I guess I just want you to know
I know how you feel
I know that impossible feeling,
The feeling that it's just too hard

Just please keep going
One second at a time

"He gives strength to the weary,
and increased the power of the weak
Even youths grow tired and weary,
and young men stumble and fall;
but those who hope in the Lord
will renew their strength
they will soar on wings like eagles
they will run and not grow weary
they will walk and not be faint."
-Is.40:29-31

"...do not fear, for I am with you,do not be dismayed, for
I am your God,I will strengthen you and help you I will
uphold you with my righteous right hand."
-Is41:10

Trust Yourself

Does society care?
Do the police care?
Do churches care?
Do Christians care?

Doesn't seem like it.
Doesn't feel like it.
Police need too much proof.
Or they say the victim is over 21--forget it!
While they wait for proof
spirits, souls, lives
are destroyed.
Christian friends
prefer to believe that he
couldn't do it
It doesn't fit into their nice
little Christian view of the
world.
Family-
Well they'll destroy you
before they let you wreck
their perfect family.

So what if I'm over 21!
Emotionally I'm 8 years old!
Society doesn't care
how fathers treat their children.
We are just something for
them to use.

Society doesn't care
They'd rather deny it
then deal with it.
Blame the victim.

But God,

It's destroying me
relationships....
And I know I could abuse....
God, I could abuse!
kill me if I try
stop me
Don't let me hurt a child!

Trust Yourself

I am 29 year old
I am a survivor/victim of incest.
I am a sex addict
I have a difficult time with relationships.
I could abuse a child.
I doubt I am capable
of a healthy relationship.
I doubt I am capable
of a healthy marriage.
Yet the law says that my
abuse was too long ago.
they wouldn't punish my father
But look at me
look at what he has done to me.
look at what he has caused!
look at the devastation!
yet it doesn't matter.

God is the only One who will
punish him.

Nobody will touch it!
Damn them!
A child tonight sleeps in fear of
his/her father and nobody can
stop it!
Damn!
Damn!
A little kid waits for daddy to come
and use his/her body for sex.
And no adult will help.
Can help
God, can I help?
What can I do?
Show me
Please
God, stop that kids hurt

You know, that is why they
think they can get away with it
Why they do it
They know it doesn't matter
Society doesn't care
You want to use your kid for sex?
No problem
If he/she is young enough
he/she can't testify
If he/she is older
Its his/her word against yours
Or they'll blame the kid for it.
Are you active in church?
An elder?
Or respected in the community?
Don't worry about it!
Even if the kid tells
nobody will believe him/her.
Or use the kid next door
a student
or your niece
If they don't live in your house it's
even better
It's not important enough
Or let's just keep it in the family.
Doesn't matter
Nobody cares

You want to use your kid
a kid
for sex?

Why do we wonder why
people do this?
We allow it
We ignore it
We protect the guilty

Trust Yourself

and persecute the innocent
We let it happen
And each time it happens
we set up another generation
for heartache and pain

And, I wonder,
do we even care?!

It's like running into a brick wall
He won't give
So I must fly
I must fight
Fight the bitch,
fight the bastard
I will win daddy
I will win Bastard!

God, Why God?!
I read his letters
I hear his voice
Nothing has changed
I am trying to ram down a brick wall
God, It doesn't give!
Makes me so angry
So angry
So angry
Right has to win dad
I have to fight him
I have to fight the lie
I have to fight him
I can't let him win.

Trust Yourself

How am I doing?
I don't know
I think I'm doing OK
I feel fairly calm
Almost too calm
Guess I've just got used to living on the edge of hell
I pretend
I just don't think about the insanity I'm living in
I try to write about this - I can't
I feel I should have died back there
I want to work at this
She wants to talk
I want her to talk to you
Talk to her she knows the answers
I don't

How do I feel ?
Why can't I talk
I feel kinda like...
How do I describe it?
None of the words are right
Dead
Cold
Like I may never go to church again
Like I want to say my feelings
But I don't think anybody will listen
I can't talk any more nobody can listen
I am dead inside
No feeling inside
I will disappear soon

Trust Yourself

They sit there
They act so concerned
and kind
I hate them so much
They look so damn good
If you all are right
and I am wrong...
Why...
am I addicted to sex?
do I fear men?
do I fear people?
do I have so much trouble with relationships?
do I have the nervous laugh?
(this bubbly personality that makes people think I'm
so happy?)
do I have flashbacks of abuse?
do the personalities remember?
am I afraid of spiders?
do I freak out at the doctor's exam (particularly pelvic)?
can't I trust anybody?
am I afraid to look anybody in the eye?
have I blocked out _____ memories?
do I have so many traits that are also seen in incest
victims?
don't I have any feelings?
don't I have any boundaries?
don't I know how to act in social situations?
(am so uncomfortable in them)
am I so immature?
do I know I've been raped?
do I know I've had a penis in my mouth?
do I know I've had a penis in my vagina?
do I feel I'm supposed to perform oral sex on men?
(out of nowhere I've got the urge.)
didn't I get the nurturing I needed?
have I been searching for a mother all my life?

do I hate communion?
do I feel guilty?
Did I make this all up?
Why...
is Joyce afraid of knives?
do the personalities seem to exist?
What about my flashback of dad with the yardstick and the
evil in his eyes?
Why...
do the personalities insist that he did it?
the anger
do I have the fear when I lay in bed at night-I guess
that something will get me?
if they all insist that they aren't perfect-why did I get
the feeling they think/act like they are?
do other people/friends see it too--that they seem to think
they are perfect?
does some of this feel true?
do I hate myself?
have I wanted to die?
am I afraid to cry?
do my friends see symptoms of sexual abuse in me, some even
before I told them? (they say, Violet I understand
you now!)
do I startle so easy?
do I always have to be in control?
does this seem to explain so many little traits I have
seen in my life and childhood if it's not true?
can't I keep my mouth shut?
do I gag when I brush my teeth?
am I afraid of chemicals?
do I expect to be hit if I cry?
(to be punished)
do I believe anything bad that happens to me I deserve?

Trust Yourself

If I am telling the truth...
Why...
don't I fit all the criteria of MPD if I am?
don't I believe all my stories are true - how do I tell
what is true?
(Dad raped me is true)
do some of the stories seem they are too bizarre?!

I do feel I need a good reason to have/deserve love.
that I need a good story so that people will love me, be
interested in me.
Why do I have this nagging feeling that I made it all up
to
please Jamie? But all of it?
I have made some of it up but not all

Why can't I settle this?
Maybe I just want love attention, justification.....

If I look at what I see, as the facts...
I am very angry at him
at them
I tend to believe he is guilty and I am right.

I don't deserve to be right.
That may be the final reason that I can't say it happened
- part
of me believes I am right but part of me won't accept it -
she believes I am lying and don't deserve to be right -
to be believed
We have never been believed before...
There is something more here...
something I am not getting to...
something important...

Why...

would I wreak all this havoc on my family if I'm not right?
can't they give me a reasonable explanation for my
differentness?

I believe,
looking at the evidence
after meeting with Jamie H., Dad, Nora, and Dr. DeRat,
I believe I didn't make this up
I believe I am right
Still so many questions
But the basics are right
I was abused sexually, emotionally, and probably
physically

If I am lying,
Why...
do I want to turn my back on my family?
would I almost prefer to never see them again?
was my fantasy as a child to get away from them?

to know...
to feel...
That I am right
To feel it in my mouth
the body of the person/child
It's an awful feeling
Awful is such a mild word
Kind word for what they did
ripping...bodies? flesh?
Hear, imagine bones cracking
to know we ate people/kids
too Awful.
to feel the feeling that tell me...
I was a part of the cult
I belonged to him (Satan)
to know, even for a second
That it's true

Trust Yourself

That it feels real

I want somebody to know me
To know what bugs me
To see the little things that I think are funny
But that will never happen
People don't love like that
I'm so scared
So much pain
I hate trying to describe it
Because describing it is useless

I wander through the field,
and pick through the piles
thrown around of half remembered memories and
theories.
I wonder which is true
which is made up by an overactive imagination
and a kid just crying for attention.
I believe/know/feel d. raped me...
or at least we had...I performed oral sex on him.
I believe/know/feel I have performed
oral sex on at least one little girl.
I wonder...I pick up this memory or that one.
I throw them back down...
I search for the truth.
I run from the truth
-the fear that I just made it all up to please J.,
to feel important
to feel special.
I feel some of it...I know it's true
...I fear...I long for relief and yet I run from relief.
I believe/know we ate dead bodies at Banquets
That stuff is so hard to talk about
I wonder who is involved
I run from the truth
the fear that the unspeakable is true
and I haven't made it up.
Am I the only one out there
who ever lived through this stuff?!
God!, they look soo good
My memories sound so crazy
I pick through the trash and I wonder
I fear both possible answers.
God, give me the courage to face the answer
-whatever it is.
I don't have it
I just don't have it.
I don't have the courage to let go of the control and

Trust Yourself

remember.

I can't listen
When people want to deny
When they insist on staying in their safe little world
You can deny we exist
It's said that is your option
I don't have that luxury
It was stolen from us years ago
We don't have the option to not believe

He holds the leash
I am the black dog
He jerks the choke chain
Because I'm getting out of line
It's the only power he has left
He has to keep the dog in line
He has to keep the dog from biting him
He jerks the choke chain
It hurts
What do I do?
Accept that he knows best?
Or rip the leash out of his hand?
There is only one answer

I am free!
I am a person
I exist
I have a body
It exists in space
I exist in space
I exist without dad!
I exist without dad!
My body moves
It works
I can do what I want to do
It's allowed
I don't have to ask dad
It's allowed
What I am is OK
I look down at my body
It's real
It moves and works
look at me
I am here
I take up space
I exist!
I am here!
Alone
Without dad
I pay my own bills
They have my name on them!
They are mine!
I do things
I can do things without dad
It's OK
It's good
I exist.
I am real
Look, I have a car
I am a real person
I bought a car

Trust Yourself

I, Alexandria
exist, am alive,
existing without
Dad
Wow
absolutely Wild!
Never thought it could happen!

Rage
Burning fire
Red and Black
Hatred
Get out of my life Dad...
Rage
At the abandonment
of Mom.
of Joyce.
At the father who abused me
Burning, Murderous Rage
Hate
Pain
at the abandonment
of Jamie
of Mom
of dad
of Geoff
of the church
of Christians
of society
Rage......

Trust Yourself

I am a jellyfish
That sea creature that throws ink
Out of its body
To make attackers think that
The black blob is the animal
While the fish has actually left the area

I send out the laughing girl
And I go away
So nobody can hurt me
Who is the real person?

She says God can change me
she talks about me honoring my father
she says I have people and Satan leading me astray
She feel she is supposed to show me the better way
That God is leading her to tell me these things
Seems like" God" is always leading somebody to talk to me
Why is she so darn sure she is right?!
She says she is saying these things
Because she loves me
That is what they always say
God is telling them to tell me things
They all have this hot line to God that I don't have...
I'm sorry -- I don't think so

Trust Yourself

the silent screams
I scream yet nobody hears
I/She screamed and nobody heard
Only Satan
I scream, does even God hear?
The pain
I hate her for leaving me.
You are just like mom
You don't help
She didn't help
She just watched them destroy me.

Daddy please be my daddy
Please let me be your little girl
Daddy hold me
Let it be OK daddy please please don't hurt me
Daddy please
Please be my daddy
Why can't you be my daddy?

Trust Yourself

God, here I am
little Ruth
Feels like I'm standing against my family
Standing for the truth
Am I?
Or am I crazy?
Or just stubborn?
God, I wish I knew
Am I noble?
Just desperate.
God,
am I doing right?
I think I am.
God, who am I to be fighting this fight?
I am nobody
I am the baby
Why am I the one fighting for the truth?

I know that I ask too much
Have to please them
Have to give up my dream of love
Kill the child that wants love
It doesn't exist
She wants too much, she won't be satisfied
She will not get enough
Is it possible to satisfy her longing?

Trust Yourself

First day of new term
I look around the classroom
I wonder...
They all sit there looking like students
reading the paper, etc.
I don't feel like a student
How can school be important?!
My family is accusing me of...
having delusions
School?!
What's that?!
I'm fighting for my life!

There is a part of me
that is sure I'm wrong
That lives in fear of being found out
Why is that?
I think
I know I'm right
But d. walks into the room
And I deny it all

I see the circumstantial evidence
I know the feeling inside
that I can't ask forgiveness
I think it's because I'm right

But I hear this voice that can't give in
she can't apologize
she isn't wrong

Am I choosing to listen to her
because it's easier?
easier than asking forgiveness
when I'm truly not sure
(she gets angry when I say that)
because she is right
When I believe
then I have the energy to fight
to live
If I don't believe
I can't go on
there will be no reason for me to live.
I think I was put on earth to fight
to start a fight against the cult

Do I live in a reality
or a myth?

Trust Yourself

Where is reality?

When I try to remember
I feel so crazy
I remember the evilness
the blackness
I can almost touch it
I believe I am right
And know I must be crazy
Because I believe it

Did my baby live?
Did I eat them
God I ate babies
did I eat Peter?
God...

Its so awful
We ate children
I read what I've written and know I'm right
The way I express it
I can feel the truth
I know I am right.

Trust Yourself

I hate the fight
to have to fight not cutting
to have to fight, to deal
with the confusion
to deal with the anger
to know all this is true
God, I hate it
I hate the truth
It hurts so bad
I hate it

What is Christmas?
A time for families?
What a joke!
Yes, Christmas is a time for families
A time for tradition

All my life
I've always known I'd never give up my traditions
--my family.
But it doesn't matter any more
It's too late
It's gone
Too much has happened
I have lost my family.

We found the tree
And gathered borrowed ornaments
When we finished,
We had a tree that didn't look bad

It reminds me of my life
I've taken the castaway parts,
I've taken the trash they've given me...
And I've done my best
And am making
A life that isn't that bad.

Trust Yourself

For the first time in years
I almost feel peace
I feel a calm
Happy almost

What is it?
Why?
It comes with beginning to accept...
Accept that I am right
That my memories are true
That it is OK to feel the pain
the rejection
the hate and fear,
fear that all of my horrible,
awful memories are true
I am allowed to be right
I am allowed to feel the pain
I am allowed to believe
I am right
I, Alexandria Wesley, am a
Satanic ritual abuse victim/survivor

Heading home
Going back to the plastic world
it's all just a fake world
a cover up
a mock up
so that nobody sees underneath
to the blackness
the blackness is going to get me
Is the blackness going to get me?
I'd like to drop a bomb
The words I know the truth
And watch it destroy the world
fragile, plastic world they've constructed
Who cares what it destroys?
Unless it hurts the children

Trust Yourself

Fathers Day
A day to honour fathers for all
they do for their children.
Yea, my father has done an awful lot for me.
So why don't I feel like celebrating him?
I used to know that I could never thank him enough
Now I know...
I hate him
How do I say it--can I say it?
Fathers Day
Happy Fathers Day, Dad
Thank you for raping me?

I'm finding me
I'm finding me
I'm finding out God loves me
I'm discovering that I exist
I'm discovering that it's OK to be me
It's OK to want what I want
My opinions are allowed to exist
It's OK to be me
It's OK to like what I like
I'm allowed to make my own decisions
I'm not just an extension of my family,
of dad
I'm finding me

www.ingramcontent.com/pod-product-compliance
Lightning Source LLC
Chambersburg PA
CBHW031934080426
42734CB00007B/676